Contents

Best-Ever Baked Beans

Beans with Smoky Canadian Bacon

- 2 cans (14½ ounces each) diced fire-roasted tomatoes, undrained
- 1 can (15 ounces) pinto beans, rinsed and drained
- 1 package (8 ounces) Canadian bacon, cut into ½-inch cubes
- ½ cup Texas-style barbecue sauce*
- 1 small onion, finely chopped
- ½ teaspoon salt
- Black pepper, to taste
- ⅛ teaspoon crushed red pepper flakes (optional)

Look for barbecue sauce with liquid smoke as an ingredient.

Combine all ingredients in **CROCK-POT®** slow cooker. Cover; cook on LOW 5 to 7 hours. Serve in bowls.

Makes 4 servings

Spicy Beans Tex-Mex

⅓ cup lentils

1⅓ cups water

5 strips bacon

1 onion, chopped

1 can (15 ounces) pinto beans, rinsed and drained

1 can (15 ounces) red kidney beans, rinsed and drained

1 can (14½ ounces) diced tomatoes, undrained

3 tablespoons ketchup

3 cloves garlic, minced

1 teaspoon chili powder

½ teaspoon ground cumin

¼ teaspoon red pepper flakes

1 bay leaf

1. Combine lentils and water in large saucepan. Boil 20 to 30 minutes; drain.

2. Cook bacon in medium skillet until crisp. Transfer to paper towels to drain. Cool, then crumble bacon. In same skillet, cook onion in bacon drippings until tender.

3. Combine lentils, bacon, onion, beans, tomatoes with juice, ketchup, garlic, chili powder, cumin, red pepper flakes and bay leaf in **CROCK-POT**® slow cooker. Cover; cook on LOW 5 to 6 hours or on HIGH 3 to 4 hours. Remove bay leaf before serving.

Makes 8 to 10 servings

Arizona Ranch Beans

1 **pound uncooked dried pinto beans**

8 **cups cool water, plus more for soaking**

½ **pound bacon, cooked and drained, reserving 2 tablespoons drippings**

1 **can (14½ ounces) tomatoes, undrained and coarsely chopped**

2 **medium onions, chopped**

2 **cloves garlic, minced**

1 **can (4 ounces) diced green chiles**

1 **teaspoon chili powder**

½ **teaspoon dried oregano**

¼ **teaspoon ground cumin**

2 **limes, cut into wedges**

1. Place beans in large bowl and add enough cool water to cover by at least 2 inches. Soak 6 to 8 hours or overnight.* Drain beans; discard water.

2. Place drained beans and 8 cups cool water in **CROCK-POT®** slow cooker. Crumble bacon into **CROCK-POT®** slow cooker and add reserved drippings. Stir in tomatoes with juice, onions, garlic, green chiles, chili powder, oregano and cumin. Cover and cook on LOW 8 to 10 hours or until beans are tender.

3. Season to taste with salt. Serve hot with lime wedges to squeeze over each serving.

Makes 6 to 8 servings

To quick soak beans, place beans in large saucepan; cover with water. Bring to a boil over high heat. Boil 2 minutes. Remove from heat; let soak, covered, 1 hour.

Five-Bean Casserole

2 **medium onions, chopped**
8 **ounces bacon, diced**
2 **cloves garlic, minced**
½ **cup packed brown sugar**
½ **cup cider vinegar**
1 **teaspoon salt**
1 **teaspoon dry mustard**
¼ **teaspoon black pepper**
2 **cans (about 15 ounces each) kidney beans, rinsed and drained**
1 **can (about 15 ounces) chickpeas, rinsed and drained**
1 **can (about 15 ounces) butter beans, rinsed and drained**
1 **can (about 15 ounces) Great Northern or cannellini beans, rinsed and drained**
1 **can (about 15 ounces) baked beans**
   Chopped green onions (optional)

1. Cook and stir onions, bacon and garlic in large skillet over medium heat until onions are tender; drain. Stir in brown sugar, vinegar, salt, mustard and pepper. Simmer over low heat 15 minutes.

2. Combine all beans in **CROCK-POT**® slow cooker. Spoon onion mixture evenly over top. Cover; cook on LOW 6 to 8 hours or on HIGH 3 to 4 hours. Serve hot, garnished with green onions.

Makes 16 servings

Baked Beans

 2 **cans (16 ounces each) baked beans**
 1 **cup ketchup**
 ½ **cup barbecue sauce**
 ½ **cup packed brown sugar**
 5 **slices bacon, chopped**
 ½ **green bell pepper, chopped**
 ½ **onion, chopped**
 1½ **teaspoons prepared mustard**
   Fresh parsley (optional)

Place all ingredients in **CROCK-POT**® slow cooker. Stir well to combine. Cover; cook on LOW 8 to 12 hours or on HIGH 3 to 4 hours. Garnish with fresh parsley.

Makes 6 to 8 servings

Lentils with Walnuts

1 cup brown lentils

1 very small onion or large shallot, chopped

1 stalk celery, trimmed and chopped

1 large carrot, chopped

¼ teaspoon crushed dried thyme

3 cups chicken broth

Salt and black pepper, to taste

¼ cup chopped walnuts

1. Combine lentils, onion, celery, carrot, thyme and broth in **CROCK-POT®** slow cooker. Cover; cook on HIGH 3 hours. (Do not overcook. Lentils should absorb most or all of broth. Slightly tilt **CROCK-POT®** slow cooker to check.)

2. Season with salt and pepper. Spoon lentils into serving bowl and sprinkle on walnuts.

Makes 4 to 6 servings

Mrs. Grady's Beans

½ **pound 90% lean ground beef**

1 **small onion, chopped**

8 **slices bacon, chopped**

1 **can (about 15 ounces) pinto beans, undrained**

1 **can (about 15 ounces) butter beans, rinsed and drained, reserving ¼ cup liquid**

1 **can (about 15 ounces) kidney beans, rinsed and drained**

¼ **cup ketchup**

2 **tablespoons molasses**

½ **teaspoon dry mustard**

½ **cup granulated sugar**

¼ **cup packed brown sugar**

1. Brown ground beef, onion and bacon in medium saucepan over high heat. Stir in beans and liquid; set aside.

2. Combine ketchup, molasses and mustard in medium bowl. Mix in sugars. Stir ketchup mixture into beef mixture; mix well. Transfer to **CROCK-POT®** slow cooker. Cover and cook on LOW 2 to 3 hours or until heated through.

Makes 6 to 8 servings

Boston Baked Beans

  2 **pounds small dry white beans**
 12 **cups water**
     Olive oil
 ¼   **cup finely chopped salt pork or thick-sliced bacon**
  1 **cup molasses**
 ½   **cup chopped onions**
 ½   **cup packed dark brown sugar**
  2 **tablespoons dry mustard**
  2 **teaspoons salt**

1. Soak beans in water in uncovered **CROCK-POT**® slow cooker overnight (or a minimum of 8 hours). After soaking, cover; cook on LOW 3 hours. Drain liquid, reserving 1 cup. Remove beans; set aside.

2. Heat oil in skillet over medium heat until hot. Add salt pork. Cook and stir 5 to 10 minutes to render fat. Remove with slotted spoon and drain on paper towels. Transfer to **CROCK-POT**® slow cooker.

3. Add reserved 1 cup cooking liquid, beans and remaining ingredients; stir well to combine. Cover; cook on LOW 10 to 12 hours or on HIGH 6 to 8 hours.

Makes 8 servings

Mama's Best Baked Beans

1 **bag (1 pound) dried Great Northern beans**
1 **package (1 pound) bacon**
5 **hot dogs, cut into ½-inch pieces**
1 **cup chopped onion**
1 **bottle (24 ounces) ketchup**
2 **cups packed dark brown sugar**

1. Soak and cook beans according to package directions. Drain and refrigerate until ready to use.

2. Cook bacon in large skillet over medium-high heat until crisp. Transfer to paper towels to drain. Cool, then crumble bacon; set aside. Discard all but 3 tablespoons bacon fat from skillet. Add hot dogs and onion. Cook and stir over medium heat until onion is tender.

3. Combine cooked beans, bacon, hot dog mixture, ketchup and brown sugar in **CROCK-POT**® slow cooker. Cover; cook on LOW 2 to 4 hours.

Makes 4 to 6 servings

Chili Barbecue Beans

1 cup dried Great Northern beans

1 cup dried red beans or dried kidney beans

1 cup dried baby lima beans

3 to 4 cups cold water, plus additional for soaking

8 slices crisp-cooked bacon, crumbled *or* 8 ounces smoked sausage, sliced

¼ cup packed brown sugar

2 tablespoons minced onion

2 beef bouillon cubes

1 teaspoon dry mustard

1 teaspoon chili powder

1 teaspoon minced garlic

½ teaspoon black pepper

¼ teaspoon red pepper flakes

2 bay leaves

1 to 1½ cups barbecue sauce

1. Place beans in large bowl and add enough cold water to cover by at least 2 inches. Soak 6 to 8 hours or overnight.* Drain beans; discard water.

2. Combine soaked beans, 3 to 4 cups cold water, bacon, brown sugar, onion, bouillon cubes, mustard, chili powder, garlic, black pepper, red pepper flakes and bay leaves in **CROCK-POT**® slow cooker. Cover and cook on LOW 8 to 10 hours or until beans are tender.

3. Stir in barbecue sauce. Cover and cook 1 hour or until heated through. Remove and discard bay leaves. Serve hot.

Makes 8 to 10 servings

To quick soak beans, place beans in large saucepan; cover with water. Bring to a boil over high heat. Boil 2 minutes. Remove from heat; let soak, covered, 1 hour.

New England Baked Beans

4 **slices uncooked bacon, chopped**

3 **cans (about 15 ounces each) Great Northern beans, rinsed and drained**

¾ **cup water**

1 **small onion, chopped**

⅓ **cup canned diced tomatoes, well drained**

3 **tablespoons packed light brown sugar**

3 **tablespoons maple syrup**

3 **tablespoons unsulphured molasses**

2 **cloves garlic, minced**

½ **teaspoon salt**

½ **teaspoon dry mustard**

⅛ **teaspoon black pepper**

½ **bay leaf**

1. Cook bacon in large skillet until almost cooked but not crispy. Drain on paper towels.

2. Combine bacon and all remaining ingredients in **CROCK-POT®** slow cooker. Cover and cook on LOW 6 to 8 hours or until mixture is thickened. Remove bay leaf before serving.

Makes 4 to 6 servings

Rice and Grain Dishes

Spinach Risotto

- 2 teaspoons butter
- 2 teaspoons olive oil
- 3 tablespoons finely chopped shallot
- 1¼ cups arborio rice
- ½ cup dry white wine
- 3 cups chicken broth
- ½ teaspoon salt
- 2 cups baby spinach
- ¼ cup grated Parmesan cheese
- 2 tablespoons pine nuts, toasted

1. Melt butter in medium skillet over medium heat; add oil. Add shallot and cook, stirring frequently, until softened but not browned.

2. Stir in rice and cook 2 to 3 minutes or until chalky and well coated. Stir in wine and cook until reduced by half. Transfer to **CROCK-POT**® slow cooker. Stir in broth and salt.

3. Cover and cook on HIGH 2 to 2½ hours or until rice is almost cooked but still contains a little liquid. Stir in spinach. Cover and cook 15 to 20 minutes or until spinach is cooked and rice is tender and creamy. Gently stir in Parmesan cheese and pine nuts just before serving.

Makes 4 servings

Vegetable Jollof Rice

1 medium eggplant (about 1¼ pounds), trimmed and cut into 1-inch cubes

1¾ teaspoons salt, divided

3 tablespoons vegetable oil, plus more as needed

1 medium onion, chopped

1 medium green bell pepper, seeded and chopped

3 medium carrots, cut into ½-inch-thick rounds

2 cloves garlic, minced

1½ cups converted rice

1 tablespoon plus ½ teaspoon chili powder

1 can (28 ounces) diced tomatoes in juice, undrained

1 can (14½ ounces) vegetable broth

> **Tip**
>
> Jollof Rice (also spelled "jolof" or sometimes "djolof") is an important dish in many West African cultures.

1. Place eggplant cubes in colander. Toss with 1 teaspoon salt. Let stand in sink for 1 hour to drain. Rinse under cold water; drain and pat dry with paper towels.

2. Heat 1 tablespoon oil in large skillet over medium-high heat. Working in batches, add eggplant to skillet and cook, turning to brown on all sides. Remove eggplant to plate as it is browned. Add additional oil, 1 tablespoon at a time, to skillet as needed to prepare all remaining batches of eggplant.

3. Wipe out skillet with paper towels. Add another 1 tablespoon oil to skillet and heat. Add onion, bell pepper, carrots and garlic. Cook, stirring occasionally, until onion is soft but not brown. Add to **CROCK-POT®** slow cooker. Stir in rice, chili powder and remaining ¾ teaspoon salt.

4. Drain tomatoes over 1-quart measuring cup, reserving tomato juice. Add vegetable broth to tomato juice. Add additional water as needed to measure 4 cups total. Pour into **CROCK-POT®** slow cooker. Add drained tomatoes and stir to level rice; top with eggplant. Cover; cook on LOW 3½ to 4 hours or until rice is tender and liquid is absorbed. Stir well and serve hot.

Makes 6 servings

Wild Rice with Fruit and Nuts

    2 cups wild rice (or wild rice blend), rinsed*
    ½ cup dried cranberries
    ½ cup chopped raisins
    ½ cup chopped dried apricots
    ½ cup almond slivers, toasted**
    5 to 6 cups chicken broth
    1 cup orange juice
    2 tablespoons butter, melted
    1 teaspoon ground cumin
    2 green onions, thinly sliced
    2 to 3 tablespoons chopped fresh parsley
       Salt and black pepper, to taste

Do not use parboiled rice or a blend containing parboiled rice.

**To toast almonds, spread in single layer in heavy-bottomed skillet. Cook over medium heat 1 to 2 minutes, stirring frequently, until nuts are lightly browned. Remove from skillet immediately. Cool before using.*

1. Combine wild rice, cranberries, raisins, apricots and almonds in **CROCK-POT®** slow cooker.

2. Combine broth, orange juice, butter and cumin in medium bowl. Pour mixture over rice and stir to mix.

3. Cover; cook on LOW 7 hours or on HIGH 2½ to 3 hours. Stir once, adding more hot broth if necessary.

4. When rice is soft, add green onions and parsley. Adjust seasonings, if desired. Cook 10 minutes longer and serve.

Makes 6 to 8 servings

Wild Rice and Dried
Cherry Risotto

1 cup dry-roasted salted peanuts

2 tablespoons sesame oil, divided

1 cup chopped onion

6 ounces uncooked wild rice

1 cup diced carrots

1 cup chopped green or red bell pepper

½ cup dried cherries

⅛ to ¼ teaspoon red pepper flakes

4 cups hot water

¼ cup teriyaki or soy sauce

1 teaspoon salt, or to taste

1. Coat **CROCK-POT®** slow cooker with nonstick cooking spray. Heat large skillet over medium-high heat until hot. Add peanuts. Cook and stir 2 to 3 minutes or until peanuts begin to brown. Transfer peanuts to plate; set aside.

2. Heat 2 teaspoons oil in skillet until hot. Add onion. Cook and stir 6 minutes or until richly browned. Transfer to **CROCK-POT®** slow cooker.

3. Stir in wild rice, carrots, bell pepper, cherries, red pepper flakes and water. Cover; cook on HIGH 3 hours.

4. Let stand 15 minutes, uncovered, until rice absorbs liquid. Stir in teriyaki sauce, peanuts, remaining oil and salt.

Makes 8 to 10 servings

Asian Golden Barley with Cashews

2 tablespoons unsalted butter

1 cup hulled barley, sorted

3 cups vegetable broth

1 cup chopped celery

1 green bell pepper, cored, seeded and chopped

1 yellow onion, peeled and minced

1 clove garlic, minced

¼ teaspoon black pepper

¼ cup finely chopped cashews

1. Heat skillet over medium heat until hot. Add butter and barley. Cook and stir about 10 minutes or until barley is slightly browned. Transfer to **CROCK-POT®** slow cooker.

2. Add broth, celery, bell pepper, onion, garlic and black pepper. Stir well to combine. Cover; cook on LOW 4 to 5 hours or on HIGH 2 to 3 hours, or until barley is tender and liquid is absorbed.

3. To serve, garnish with cashews.

Makes 4 servings

Greek Rice

2 tablespoons butter

1¾ cups uncooked converted long-grain rice

2 cans (14 ounces each) low-sodium, fat-free chicken broth

1 teaspoon Greek seasoning

1 teaspoon ground oregano

1 cup pitted kalamata olives, drained and chopped

¾ cup chopped roasted red peppers

Crumbled feta cheese (optional)

Chopped fresh Italian parsley (optional)

Melt butter in large nonstick skillet over medium-high heat. Add rice and sauté 4 minutes or until golden brown. Transfer to **CROCK-POT**® slow cooker. Stir in chicken broth, Greek seasoning and oregano. Cover and cook on LOW 4 hours or until liquid has all been absorbed and rice is tender. Stir in olives and roasted red peppers and cook 5 minutes more. Garnish with feta and Italian parsley.

Makes 6 to 8 servings

Barley with Currants and Pine Nuts

1 **tablespoon unsalted butter**
1 **small onion, finely chopped**
½ **cup pearled barley**
2 **cups chicken broth**
½ **teaspoon salt, or to taste**
¼ **teaspoon black pepper**
⅓ **cup currants**
¼ **cup pine nuts**

1. Melt butter in small skillet over medium-high heat. Add onion. Cook and stir until lightly browned, about 2 minutes. Transfer to **CROCK-POT®** slow cooker. Add barley, broth, salt and pepper. Stir in currants. Cover; cook on LOW 3 hours.

2. Stir in pine nuts and serve immediately.

Makes 4 servings

Polenta-Style Corn Casserole

1 **can (14½ ounces) chicken broth**
½ **cup cornmeal**
1 **can (7 ounces) corn, drained**
1 **can (4 ounces) diced green chiles, drained**
¼ **cup diced red bell pepper**
½ **teaspoon salt**
¼ **teaspoon black pepper**
1 **cup (4 ounces) shredded Cheddar cheese**

Serving Suggestion

Divide cooked corn mixture into lightly greased individual ramekins or spread in pie plate; cover and refrigerate. Serve at room temperature or warm in oven or microwave.

1. Pour broth into **CROCK-POT**® slow cooker. Whisk in cornmeal. Add corn, chiles, bell pepper, salt and black pepper. Cover; cook on LOW 4 to 5 hours or on HIGH 2 to 3 hours.

2. Stir in cheese. Continue cooking, uncovered, 15 to 30 minutes or until cheese melts.

Makes 6 servings

Spanish Paella-Style Rice

2 cans (14½ ounces each) chicken broth

1½ cups uncooked converted long-grain rice

1 small red bell pepper, diced

⅓ cup dry white wine or water

½ teaspoon saffron threads, crushed or
½ teaspoon ground turmeric

⅛ teaspoon red pepper flakes

½ cup frozen peas, thawed

Salt, to taste

Tip

Paella can contain a variety of meats as well. For more authenticity—and to turn this dish into a delicious main course—add ½ cup cooked ham, chicken, chorizo or seafood when you add the peas.

1. Combine broth, rice, bell pepper, wine, saffron and red pepper flakes in **CROCK-POT®** slow cooker; mix well. Cover; cook on LOW 4 hours or until liquid is absorbed.

2. Stir in peas. Cover; cook 15 to 30 minutes or until peas are hot. Season with salt.

Makes 6 servings

Artichoke and Tomato Paella

4 cups vegetable broth

2 cups converted white rice

5 ounces (half 10-ounce package) frozen chopped spinach, thawed and drained

1 green bell pepper, cored, seeded and chopped

1 medium ripe tomato, sliced into wedges

1 medium yellow onion, chopped

1 medium carrot, peeled and diced

3 cloves garlic, minced

1 tablespoon minced flat-leaf parsley

1 teaspoon salt

½ teaspoon black pepper

1 can (13¾ ounces) artichoke hearts, quartered, rinsed and well-drained

½ cup frozen peas

1. Combine broth, rice, spinach, bell pepper, tomato, onion, carrot, garlic, parsley, salt and black pepper in **CROCK-POT**® slow cooker. Mix thoroughly. Cover; cook on LOW 4 hours or on HIGH 2 hours.

2. Before serving, add artichoke hearts and peas. Cover; cook on HIGH 15 minutes. Mix well before serving.

Makes 8 servings

Easy Dirty Rice

½ pound bulk Italian sausage
2 cups water
1 cup uncooked long-grain rice
1 large onion, finely chopped
1 large green bell pepper, finely chopped
½ cup finely chopped celery
1½ teaspoons salt
½ teaspoon ground red pepper
½ cup chopped fresh parsley

1. Brown sausage in skillet 6 to 8 minutes over medium-high heat, stirring to break up meat. Drain fat. Place sausage in **CROCK-POT®** slow cooker.

2. Stir in all remaining ingredients except parsley. Cover; cook on LOW 2 hours. Stir in parsley.

Makes 4 servings

Garlic and Herb Polenta

3 tablespoons butter, divided

8 cups water

2 cups yellow cornmeal

2 teaspoons finely minced garlic

2 teaspoons salt

3 tablespoons chopped fresh herbs such as parsley, chives, thyme or chervil (or a combination of any of these)

Tip

Polenta may also be poured into a greased pan and allowed to cool until set. Cut into squares (or slice as desired) to serve. For even more great flavor, chill polenta slices until firm, then grill or fry until golden brown.

Butter inside of **CROCK-POT**® slow cooker with 1 tablespoon butter. Add water, cornmeal, garlic, salt and remaining 2 tablespoons butter; stir. Cover and cook on LOW 4 hours or on HIGH 3 hours, stirring occasionally. Stir in chopped herbs just before serving.

Makes 6 servings

Tasty Veggies

Braised Sweet and Sour Cabbage and Apples

- 2 tablespoons unsalted butter
- 6 cups coarsely shredded red cabbage
- 1 large sweet apple, peeled, cored and cut into bite-size pieces
- 3 whole cloves
- ½ cup raisins
- ½ cup apple cider
- 3 tablespoons cider vinegar, divided
- 2 tablespoons packed dark brown sugar
- ½ teaspoon salt
- ¼ teaspoon black pepper

1. Melt butter in very large skillet or shallow pot over medium heat. Add cabbage. Cook and stir 3 minutes until cabbage is glossy. Transfer to **CROCK-POT**® slow cooker.

2. Add apple, cloves, raisins, apple cider, 2 tablespoons vinegar, brown sugar, salt and pepper. Cover; cook on LOW 2½ to 3 hours.

3. To serve, remove cloves and stir in remaining 1 tablespoon vinegar.

Makes 4 to 6 servings

Tarragon Carrots in White Wine

½ cup chicken broth
½ cup dry white wine
1 tablespoon lemon juice
1 tablespoon minced fresh tarragon
2 teaspoons finely chopped green onions
1½ teaspoons chopped flat-leaf parsley
1 clove garlic, minced
1 teaspoon salt
8 medium carrots, peeled and cut into matchsticks
2 tablespoons melba toast, crushed
2 tablespoons cold water

1. Combine broth, wine, lemon juice, tarragon, onions, parsley, garlic and salt in **CROCK-POT®** slow cooker. Add carrots; stir well to combine. Cover; cook on LOW 2½ to 3 hours or on HIGH 1½ to 2 hours.

2. Turn **CROCK-POT®** slow cooker to HIGH. Dissolve toast crumbs in water and add to carrots. Cover; cook 10 minutes longer or until thickened.

Makes 6 to 8 servings

Tip

Fresh herbs like tarragon are very perishable, so purchase them in small amounts. For short-term storage, place the herb stems in water and cover the leaves loosely with a plastic bag or plastic wrap and store in the refrigerator. This will keep tarragon at its best for up to five days.

Supper Squash Medley

2 **butternut squash, peeled, seeded and diced**
1 **can (28 ounces) tomatoes, undrained**
1 **can (15 ounces) corn, drained**
2 **onions, chopped**
2 **green bell peppers, chopped**
2 **teaspoons minced garlic**
2 **green chiles, chopped**
1 **cup chicken broth**
1 **teaspoon salt**
½ **teaspoon black pepper**
1 **can (6 ounces) tomato paste**

1. Combine squash, tomatoes with juice, corn, onions, bell peppers, garlic, chiles, broth, salt and black pepper in **CROCK-POT**® slow cooker. Cover; cook on LOW 6 hours.

2. Remove about ½ cup cooking liquid and blend with tomato paste. Add back to **CROCK-POT**® slow cooker and stir well. Cook 30 minutes or until mixture is slightly thickened and heated through.

Makes 8 to 10 servings

Tip

To prepare butternut squash, first rinse with cold running water and dry. Cut squash in half lengthwise. Scoop out seeds (use sturdy metal spoon or ice cream scoop) and discard. Cut into 1-inch slices and peel with thin paring knife (squash skin is generally too thick for most vegetable peelers). Cut slices into cubes.

Manchego Eggplant

4 large eggplants
1 cup all-purpose flour
2 tablespoons olive oil
1 jar (25½ ounces) roasted garlic flavor pasta sauce
2 tablespoons Italian seasoning
1 cup (4 ounces) grated manchego cheese
1 jar (24 ounces) roasted eggplant flavor marinara

1. Peel eggplants and slice horizontally into ¾-inch-thick pieces. Place flour in shallow bowl. Dredge each slice of eggplant in flour to coat.

2. Heat oil in large skillet over medium-high heat. In batches, lightly brown eggplant on both sides.

3. Pour thin layer of roasted garlic flavor pasta sauce into bottom of **CROCK-POT®** slow cooker. Top with eggplant slices, Italian seasoning, manchego cheese and roasted eggplant flavor marinara. Repeat layers until all ingredients have been used.

4. Cover and cook on HIGH 2 hours.

Makes 8 to 10 servings

Tip

When purchasing eggplant, choose a firm eggplant that feels heavy for its size, with a tight, glossy, deeply colored skin. The stem should be bright green. Dull skin and rust-colored spots are a sign of old age. Refrigerate unwashed eggplant in a plastic bag for up to five days.

Scalloped Tomatoes and Corn

1 can (15 ounces) cream-style corn

1 can (14½ ounces) diced tomatoes, undrained

¾ cup saltine or soda cracker crumbs

1 egg, lightly beaten

2 teaspoons sugar

¾ teaspoon black pepper

Chopped fresh tomatoes

Chopped fresh parsley

Note

Fresh tomatoes are available all year, although locally grown summer tomatoes are superior to all others. Depending on the area, tomato season usually begins in mid-summer and lasts through September.

Combine corn, tomatoes with juice, cracker crumbs, egg, sugar and pepper in **CROCK-POT®** slow cooker; mix well. Cover; cook on LOW 4 to 6 hours or until done. Sprinkle with tomatoes and parsley before serving.

Makes 4 to 6 servings

Braised Beets with Cranberries

2½ **pounds medium beets, peeled and cut in sixths**

½ **cup sweetened dried cranberries**

1 **cup cranberry juice**

2 **tablespoons honey**

2 **tablespoons butter, cut into small pieces**

2 **tablespoons quick-cooking tapioca**

½ **teaspoon salt**

⅓ **cup crumbled blue cheese (optional)**

Orange peel, thinly sliced or grated (optional)

1. Combine beets, cranberries, cranberry juice, honey, butter, tapioca and salt in **CROCK-POT®** slow cooker. Cover and cook on LOW 7 to 8 hours or until beets are tender.

2. Transfer beets to serving bowl with slotted spoon. Pour half of cooking liquid over beets. Serve warm, at room temperature or chilled and sprinkled with blue cheese and orange peel, if desired.

Makes 6 to 8 servings

Corn on the Cob with Garlic Herb Butter

½ **cup (1 stick) unsalted butter, at room temperature**
3 **to 4 cloves garlic, minced**
2 **tablespoons finely minced fresh parsley**
4 **to 5 ears of corn, husked**
   Salt and freshly ground black pepper, to taste

1. Thoroughly mix butter, garlic and parsley in small bowl.

2. Place each ear of corn on a piece of aluminum foil and generously spread butter mixture on each ear. Season corn with salt and pepper and tightly seal foil. Place corn in **CROCK-POT®** slow cooker; overlap ears, if necessary. Add enough water to come one-fourth of the way up each ear.

3. Cover; cook on LOW 4 to 5 hours or on HIGH 2 to 2½ hours or until done.

Makes 4 to 5 servings

Old-Fashioned Sauerkraut

8 slices bacon, chopped
2 pounds sauerkraut
1 large head cabbage or 2 small heads cabbage
2½ cups chopped onions
¼ cup (½ stick) butter
2 tablespoons sugar
1 teaspoon salt
1 teaspoon black pepper

Note

Add your favorite bratwurst, knockwurst or other sausage to this recipe to make an entire meal.

1. Heat skillet over medium heat until hot. Cook and stir bacon until crisp. Remove skillet from heat and set aside. (Do not drain bacon fat.)

2. Place sauerkraut, cabbage, onions, butter, sugar, salt and pepper in **CROCK-POT®** slow cooker. Pour bacon and bacon fat over sauerkraut mixture. Cover; cook on LOW 4 to 5 hours or on HIGH 1 to 3 hours.

Makes 8 to 10 servings

Lemon and Tangerine Glazed Carrots

  6 **cups sliced carrots**
1½ **cups apple juice**
  6 **tablespoons butter**
¼ **cup packed brown sugar**
  2 **tablespoons grated lemon peel**
  2 **tablespoons grated tangerine peel**
½ **teaspoon salt**
     Fresh parsley, chopped (optional)

Combine all ingredients except parsley in **CROCK-POT®** slow cooker. Cover; cook on LOW 4 to 5 hours or on HIGH 1 to 3 hours. Garnish with chopped parsley.

Makes 10 to 12 servings

Red Cabbage and Apples

1 **small head red cabbage, cored and thinly sliced**
3 **medium apples, peeled and grated**
¾ **cup sugar**
½ **cup red wine vinegar**
1 **teaspoon ground cloves**
1 **cup crisp-cooked and crumbled bacon (optional)**
 Fresh apple slices (optional)

Combine cabbage, grated apples, sugar, vinegar and cloves in **CROCK-POT®** slow cooker. Cover; cook on HIGH 6 hours, stirring after 3 hours. To serve, sprinkle with bacon, if desired, and garnish with apple slices.

Makes 4 to 6 servings

Creamy Curried Spinach

3 **packages (10 ounces each) frozen spinach, thawed**
1 **onion, chopped**
4 **teaspoons minced garlic**
2 **tablespoons curry powder**
2 **tablespoons butter, melted**
¼ **cup chicken broth**
¼ **cup heavy cream**
1 **teaspoon lemon juice**

Combine spinach, onion, garlic, curry powder, butter and broth in **CROCK-POT®** slow cooker. Cover; cook on LOW 3 to 4 hours or on HIGH 2 hours or until done. Stir in cream and lemon juice 30 minutes before end of cooking time.

Makes 6 to 8 servings

Winter Squash and Apples

1 teaspoon salt
½ teaspoon black pepper
1 butternut squash (about 2 pounds), peeled and seeded
2 apples, cored and cut into slices
1 medium onion, quartered and sliced
1½ tablespoons butter

1. Combine salt and pepper in small bowl; set aside.

2. Cut squash into 2-inch pieces; place in **CROCK-POT**® slow cooker. Add apples and onion. Sprinkle with salt mixture; stir well. Cover; cook on LOW 6 to 7 hours or until vegetables are tender.

3. Just before serving, stir in butter and season to taste with additional salt and pepper.

Makes 4 to 6 servings

Potatoes on the Side

Bacon and Cheese
Brunch Potatoes

3 medium russet potatoes (about 2 pounds), peeled and cut into 1-inch dice
1 cup chopped onion
½ teaspoon seasoned salt
4 slices crisply cooked bacon, crumbled
1 cup (4 ounces) shredded sharp Cheddar cheese
1 tablespoon water or chicken broth

1. Coat **CROCK-POT**® slow cooker with cooking spray. Place half of potatoes in **CROCK-POT**® slow cooker. Sprinkle half of onion and seasoned salt over potatoes; top with half of bacon and cheese. Repeat layers, ending with cheese. Sprinkle water over top.

2. Cover; cook on LOW 6 hours or on HIGH 3½ hours, or until potatoes and onion are tender. Stir gently to mix and serve hot.

Makes 6 servings

Lemon-Mint Red Potatoes

2   **pounds new red potatoes**

3   **tablespoons extra-virgin olive oil**

¾   **teaspoon dried Greek seasoning or dried oregano leaves**

¼   **teaspoon garlic powder**

1   **teaspoon salt**

¼   **teaspoon black pepper**

2   **tablespoons lemon juice**

1   **teaspoon grated lemon peel**

2   **tablespoons butter**

¼   **cup chopped fresh mint leaves, divided**

1. Coat inside of **CROCK-POT**® slow cooker with nonstick cooking spray. Add potatoes and oil, stirring gently to coat. Sprinkle with Greek seasoning, garlic powder, salt and pepper. Cover and cook on LOW 7 hours or on HIGH 4 hours.

2. Stir in lemon juice, lemon peel, butter and 2 tablespoons mint. Stir until butter is completely melted. Cover and cook 15 minutes to allow flavors to blend. Sprinkle with remaining mint.

Makes 4 servings

Tip

It's easy to prepare these potatoes ahead of time. Simply follow the recipe and then turn off the heat. Let it stand at room temperature for up to 2 hours. You may reheat or serve the potatoes at room temperature.

Mediterranean Red Potatoes

3 medium red potatoes, cut into bite-size pieces
⅔ cup fresh or frozen pearl onions
    Garlic-flavored cooking spray
¾ teaspoon dried Italian seasoning
¼ teaspoon black pepper
1 small tomato, seeded and chopped
2 ounces (½ cup) feta cheese, crumbled
2 tablespoons chopped black olives

1. Place potatoes and onions in 1½-quart soufflé dish. Spray with cooking spray; toss to coat. Add Italian seasoning and pepper; mix well. Cover dish tightly with foil.

2. Tear off three 18×3-inch strips of heavy-duty foil. Cross strips to resemble wheel spokes. Place soufflé dish in center of strips. Pull foil strips up and over dish and place dish into **CROCK-POT®** slow cooker.

3. Pour hot water into **CROCK-POT®** slow cooker to about 1½ inches from top of soufflé dish. Cover; cook on LOW 7 to 8 hours.

4. Use foil handles to lift dish out of **CROCK-POT®** slow cooker. Stir chopped tomato, feta cheese and olives into potato mixture.

Makes 4 servings

Tip

Cooking times are guidelines. **CROCK-POT®** slow cookers, just like ovens, cook differently depending on the recipe size and the individual slow cooker. Always check for doneness before serving.

Swiss Cheese Scalloped Potatoes

  2 pounds baking potatoes, peeled and thinly sliced
  ½ cup finely chopped yellow onion
  ¼ teaspoon salt
  ¼ teaspoon ground nutmeg
  2 tablespoons butter, cut into small pieces
  ½ cup milk
  2 tablespoons all-purpose flour
  3 ounces Swiss cheese slices, torn into small pieces
  ¼ cup finely chopped green onions (optional)

1. Layer half the potatoes, ¼ cup onion, ⅛ teaspoon salt, ⅛ teaspoon nutmeg and 1 tablespoon butter in **CROCK-POT**® slow cooker. Repeat layers. Cover; cook on LOW 7 hours or on HIGH 4 hours.

2. Remove potatoes with slotted spoon to serving dish and cover with foil to keep warm.

3. Blend milk and flour in small bowl until smooth. Stir mixture into cooking liquid. Add cheese; stir to combine. Turn **CROCK-POT**® slow cooker to HIGH. Cover; cook until slightly thickened, about 10 minutes. Stir. Pour cheese mixture over potatoes and serve. Garnish with chopped green onions.

Makes 5 to 6 servings

Tip

Don't add water to the **CROCK-POT**® slow cooker unless a recipe specifically says so. Foods don't lose much moisture during slow cooking, so follow recipe guidelines.

Rustic Cheddar Mashed Potatoes

2 pounds russet potatoes, peeled and diced

1 cup water

⅓ cup butter, cut into small pieces

½ to ¾ cup milk

1¼ teaspoons salt

½ teaspoon black pepper

½ cup finely chopped green onions

½ to ¾ cup (2 to 3 ounces) shredded Cheddar cheese

1. Combine potatoes and water in **CROCK-POT**® slow cooker; dot with butter. Cover; cook on LOW 6 hours or on HIGH 3 hours, or until potatoes are tender. Transfer potatoes to large mixing bowl.

2. Using electric mixer at medium speed, whip potatoes until well blended. Add milk, salt and pepper; whip until well blended.

3. Stir in green onions and cheese; cover. Let stand 15 minutes to allow flavors to blend and cheese to melt.

Makes 8 servings

Blue Cheese Potatoes

2 pounds red potatoes, peeled and cut into ½-inch pieces

1¼ cups chopped green onions, divided

2 tablespoons olive oil, divided

1 teaspoon dried basil

½ teaspoon salt

¼ teaspoon black pepper

2 ounces crumbled blue cheese

1. Layer potatoes, 1 cup green onions, 1 tablespoon oil, basil, salt and pepper in **CROCK-POT**® slow cooker. Cover; cook on LOW 7 hours or on HIGH 4 hours.

2. Turn **CROCK-POT**® slow cooker to HIGH. Gently stir in cheese and remaining 1 tablespoon oil. Cook 5 minutes longer to allow flavors to blend. Transfer potatoes to serving platter and top with remaining ¼ cup green onions.

Makes 5 servings

Parmesan Potato Wedges

2   **pounds red potatoes, cut into ½-inch wedges**

¼   **cup finely chopped yellow onion**

1½   **teaspoons dried oregano**

½   **teaspoon salt**

¼   **teaspoon black pepper, or to taste**

2   **tablespoons butter, cut into ⅛-inch pieces**

¼   **cup (1 ounce) grated Parmesan cheese**

Layer potatoes, onion, oregano, salt, pepper and butter in **CROCK-POT®** slow cooker. Cover; cook on HIGH 4 hours. Transfer potatoes to serving platter and sprinkle with cheese.

Makes 6 servings

Orange-Spiced Sweet Potatoes

2 pounds sweet potatoes, peeled and diced

½ cup packed dark brown sugar

½ cup (1 stick) butter, cut into small pieces

1 teaspoon ground cinnamon

½ teaspoon ground nutmeg

½ teaspoon grated orange peel

Juice of 1 medium orange

¼ teaspoon salt

1 teaspoon vanilla

Chopped toasted pecans (optional)

Tip

For a creamy variation, mash potatoes with a hand masher or electric mixer, and add ¼ cup milk or whipping cream. Sprinkle with cinnamon-sugar and sprinkle on toasted pecans, if desired.

Place all ingredients except pecans in **CROCK-POT®** slow cooker. Cover; cook on LOW 4 hours or on HIGH 2 hours or until potatoes are tender. Sprinkle with pecans before serving, if desired.

Makes 8 servings

Deluxe Potato Casserole

1 can (10¾ ounces) condensed cream of chicken soup, undiluted
1 container (8 ounces) sour cream
¼ cup chopped onion
¼ cup (½ stick) plus 3 tablespoons melted butter, divided
1 teaspoon salt
2 pounds red potatoes, peeled and diced
2 cups (8 ounces) shredded Cheddar cheese
1½ to 2 cups stuffing mix

1. Combine soup, sour cream, onion, ¼ cup butter and salt in small bowl.

2. Combine potatoes and cheese in **CROCK-POT®** slow cooker. Pour soup mixture over potato mixture; mix well. Sprinkle stuffing mix over potato mixture; drizzle with remaining 3 tablespoons butter. Cover; cook on LOW 8 to 10 hours or on HIGH 5 to 6 hours, or until potatoes are tender.

Makes 8 to 10 servings

Gratin Potatoes with Asiago Cheese

6 slices bacon, cut into 1-inch pieces

6 medium baking potatoes, peeled and thinly sliced

½ cup grated Asiago cheese

Salt and black pepper, to taste

1½ cups heavy cream

1. Heat skillet over medium heat until hot. Add bacon. Cook and stir until crispy. Transfer to paper towel-lined plate with slotted spoon to drain.

2. Pour bacon fat from skillet into **CROCK-POT®** slow cooker. Layer one fourth of potatoes on bottom of **CROCK-POT®** slow cooker. Sprinkle one fourth of bacon over potatoes and top with one fourth of cheese. Add salt and pepper. Repeat layers. Pour cream over all. Cover; cook on LOW 7 to 9 hours or on HIGH 5 to 6 hours. Adjust salt and pepper, if desired.

Makes 4 to 6 servings

Scalloped Potatoes and Parsnips

 6 **tablespoons unsalted butter**
 3 **tablespoons all-purpose flour**
1¾ **cups whipping cream**
 2 **teaspoons dry mustard**
1½ **teaspoons salt**
 1 **teaspoon dried thyme**
 ½ **teaspoon black pepper**
 2 **baking potatoes, cut in half lengthwise, then crosswise into ¼-inch slices**
 2 **parsnips, cut into ¼-inch slices**
 1 **onion, chopped**
 2 **cups (8 ounces) shredded sharp Cheddar cheese**

1. To prepare cream sauce, melt butter in medium saucepan over medium-high heat. Whisk in flour; cook 1 to 2 minutes. Slowly whisk in cream, mustard, salt, thyme and pepper until smooth.

2. Place potatoes, parsnips and onion in **CROCK-POT®** slow cooker. Add cream sauce. Cover; cook on LOW 7 hours or on HIGH 3½ hours or until potatoes are tender.

3. Stir in cheese. Cover; let stand until cheese melts.

Makes 4 to 6 servings

Chunky Ranch Potatoes

3 pounds medium red potatoes, unpeeled and quartered

1 cup water

½ cup prepared ranch dressing

½ cup grated Parmesan or Cheddar cheese (optional)

¼ cup minced chives

1. Place potatoes in **CROCK-POT**® slow cooker. Add water. Cover; cook on LOW 7 to 9 hours or on HIGH 4 to 6 hours or until potatoes are tender.

2. Stir in ranch dressing, cheese, if desired, and chives. Use spoon to break potatoes into chunks. Serve hot or cold.

Makes 8 servings

Slow-Cooked Quick Breads

Skinny Corn Bread

1¼ cups all-purpose flour
¾ cup yellow cornmeal
¼ cup sugar
1 teaspoon baking powder
1 teaspoon baking soda
1 teaspoon seasoned salt
1 cup fat-free buttermilk
¼ cup cholesterol-free egg substitute
¼ cup canola oil

Tip

This recipe works best in round **CROCK-POT®** slow cookers.

1. Coat 3-quart **CROCK-POT®** slow cooker with nonstick cooking spray.

2. Sift together flour, cornmeal, sugar, baking powder, baking soda and seasoned salt in large bowl. Make well in center of dry mixture. Pour in buttermilk, egg substitute and oil. Mix in dry ingredients just until moistened. Pour mixture into **CROCK-POT®** slow cooker.

3. Cook, covered, with lid slightly ajar to allow excess moisture to escape, on LOW 3 to 4 hours or on HIGH 45 minutes to 1½ hours, or until edges are golden and knife inserted into center comes out clean. Remove insert from **CROCK-POT®** slow cooker. Cool on wire rack about 10 minutes; remove bread from insert and cool completely on rack.

Makes 8 servings

Bran Muffin Bread

2 cups all-bran cereal

2 cups whole wheat flour*

2 teaspoons baking powder

1 teaspoon baking soda

¼ teaspoon ground cinnamon

½ teaspoon salt

1 egg

1½ cups buttermilk

¼ cup molasses

¼ cup (½ stick) unsalted butter, melted

1 cup chopped walnuts

½ cup raisins

Honey butter or cream cheese (optional)

For proper texture of finished bread, spoon flour into measuring cup and level off. Do not dip into bag, pack down flour or tap on counter to level when measuring.

1. Generously butter and flour 8-cup mold that fits into 6-quart **CROCK-POT**® slow cooker; set aside. Combine cereal, flour, baking powder, baking soda, cinnamon and salt in large bowl. Stir to blend well.

2. Beat egg in medium bowl. Add buttermilk, molasses and melted butter. Mix well to blend. Add to flour mixture. Stir only until ingredients are combined. Stir in walnuts and raisins. Spoon batter into prepared mold. Cover with buttered foil, butter side down.

3. Place rack in **CROCK-POT**® slow cooker or prop up mold with a few equal-size potatoes. Pour 1 inch hot water into **CROCK-POT**® slow cooker (water should not come to top of rack). Place mold on rack. Cover; cook on LOW 3½ to 4 hours.

4. To check for doneness, lift foil. Bread should just start to pull away from sides of mold, and toothpick inserted into center of bread should come out clean. If necessary, replace foil and continue cooking 45 minutes longer.

5. Remove mold from **CROCK-POT**® slow cooker. Let stand 10 minutes. Remove foil and run rubber spatula around outer edges, lifting bottom slightly to loosen. Invert bread onto wire rack. Cool until lukewarm. Slice and serve with honey butter, if desired.

Makes 12 servings

Buttermilk Corn Bread

1½ **cups cornmeal**

½ **cup all-purpose flour**

1 **tablespoon sugar**

2 **teaspoons baking powder**

½ **teaspoon salt**

½ **teaspoon baking soda**

1½ **cups buttermilk**

2 **eggs**

¼ **cup (½ stick) butter, melted**

¼ **cup chopped jalapeño peppers, or to taste***

1 **tablespoon finely chopped pimiento or roasted red pepper**

*Jalapeño peppers can sting and irritate the skin, so wear rubber gloves when handling peppers and do not touch your eyes.

1. Coat inside of **CROCK-POT**® slow cooker with nonstick cooking spray.

2. Sift cornmeal, flour, sugar, baking powder and salt into large bowl; set aside. Stir baking soda into buttermilk in medium bowl. Add eggs; beat lightly with fork. Stir in melted butter.

3. Add buttermilk mixture, peppers and pimiento to cornmeal mixture. Mix until just blended. (Do not overmix.) Pour into prepared **CROCK-POT**® slow cooker. Cover and cook on HIGH 1½ to 2 hours.

Makes 8 servings

Whole-Grain Banana Bread

¼ cup plus 2 tablespoons wheat germ, divided

⅔ cup butter, softened

1 cup sugar

2 eggs

1 cup mashed bananas (2 to 3 bananas)

1 teaspoon vanilla

1 cup all-purpose flour

1 cup whole wheat pastry flour

1 teaspoon baking soda

½ teaspoon salt

½ cup chopped walnuts or pecans (optional)

1. Spray 1-quart casserole, soufflé dish or other high-sided baking pan with nonstick cooking spray. Sprinkle dish with 2 tablespoons wheat germ.

2. Beat ½ cup butter and sugar in large bowl with electric mixer until fluffy. Add eggs, one at a time; beat until blended. Add bananas and vanilla; beat until smooth.

3. Gradually stir in flours, remaining ¼ cup wheat germ, baking soda and salt. Stir in nuts, if desired. Pour batter into prepared dish; place in 4½-quart **CROCK-POT®** slow cooker. Cover; cook on LOW 4 to 6 hours or on HIGH 2 to 3 hours or until edges begin to brown and toothpick inserted into center comes out clean.

4. Remove dish from **CROCK-POT®** slow cooker. Cool on wire rack about 10 minutes. Remove bread from dish; cool completely on wire rack.

Makes 8 to 10 servings

Mexican Corn Bread Pudding

1   **can (14¾ ounces) cream-style corn**

2   **eggs**

1   **can (4 ounces) diced mild green chilies**

2   **tablespoons vegetable oil**

¾   **cup yellow cornmeal**

2   **tablespoons sugar**

2   **teaspoons baking powder**

¾   **teaspoon salt**

½   **cup shredded Cheddar cheese**

Coat 2-quart **CROCK-POT®** slow cooker with nonstick cooking spray. Combine corn, eggs, chilies, oil, cornmeal, sugar, baking powder and salt in medium bowl. Stir well to blend. Pour into **CROCK-POT®** slow cooker. Cover; cook on LOW 2 to 2½ hours or until center is set. Sprinkle cheese over top. Cover and let stand 5 minutes or until cheese is melted.

Makes 8 servings

Spinach Gorgonzola Corn Bread

- **2 boxes (8½ ounces each) corn bread mix**
- **3 eggs**
- **½ cup cream**
- **1 box (10 ounces) frozen chopped spinach, thawed and drained**
- **1 cup crumbled Gorgonzola**
- **1 teaspoon black pepper**
- **Paprika (optional)**

Note

Cook only on HIGH setting for proper crust and texture.

1. Coat 4½-quart **CROCK-POT®** slow cooker with nonstick cooking spray.

2. Mix all ingredients in medium bowl. Place batter in **CROCK-POT®** slow cooker. Cover; cook on HIGH 1½ hours. Sprinkle top with paprika for more colorful crust, if desired. Let bread cool completely before inverting onto serving platter.

Makes 10 to 12 servings

Gingerbread

- ½ cup (1 stick) butter, softened
- ½ cup sugar
- 1 egg, lightly beaten
- 1 cup light molasses
- 2½ cups all-purpose flour
- 1½ teaspoons baking soda
- 1 teaspoon ground cinnamon
- 2 teaspoons ground ginger
- ½ teaspoon ground cloves
- ½ teaspoon salt
- 1 cup hot water
- Whipped cream (optional)

1. Coat 4½-quart **CROCK-POT®** slow cooker with butter or nonstick cooking spray. Beat together butter and sugar in large bowl. Add egg, molasses, flour, baking soda, cinnamon, ginger, cloves and salt. Stir in hot water and mix well. Pour batter into **CROCK-POT®** slow cooker.

2. Cover; cook on HIGH 1½ to 1¾ hours or until toothpick inserted into center of cake comes out clean. Serve warm; top with whipped cream, if desired.

Makes 6 to 8 servings

Spinach Spoon Bread

1 **package (10 ounces) frozen chopped spinach, thawed and squeezed dry**
1 **red bell pepper, diced**
4 **eggs, lightly beaten**
1 **cup cottage cheese**
1 **package (5½ ounces) corn bread mix**
6 **green onions, sliced**
½ **cup (1 stick) butter, melted**
1¼ **teaspoons seasoned salt**

1. Coat **CROCK-POT®** slow cooker with nonstick cooking spray. Preheat on HIGH.

2. Combine all ingredients in large bowl; mix well. Pour batter into prepared **CROCK-POT®** slow cooker. Cook, covered, with lid slightly ajar to allow excess moisture to escape, on LOW 3 to 4 hours or on HIGH 1¾ to 2 hours, or until edges are golden and knife inserted into center of bread comes out clean.

3. Loosen edges and bottom with knife and invert onto plate. Cut into wedges to serve. Or serve bread spooned from **CROCK-POT®** slow cooker.

Makes 8 servings

Orange Cranberry-Nut Bread

2 cups all-purpose flour
1 teaspoon baking powder
½ teaspoon baking soda
¼ teaspoon salt
½ cup chopped pecans
1 cup dried cranberries
2 teaspoons dried orange peel
⅔ cup boiling water
¾ cup sugar
2 tablespoons shortening
1 egg, lightly beaten
1 teaspoon vanilla

Tip

This recipe works best in round **CROCK-POT®** slow cookers.

1. Coat 3-quart **CROCK-POT®** slow cooker with nonstick cooking spray. Blend flour, baking powder, baking soda and salt in medium bowl. Mix in pecans; set aside.

2. Combine cranberries and orange peel in separate medium bowl; pour boiling water over fruit mixture and stir. Add sugar, shortening, egg and vanilla; stir just until blended. Add flour mixture; stir just until blended.

3. Pour batter into **CROCK-POT®** slow cooker. Cover; cook on HIGH 1¼ to 1½ hours or until edges begin to brown and toothpick inserted into center comes out clean. Remove insert from **CROCK-POT®** slow cooker. Cool on wire rack about 10 minutes; remove bread from insert and cool completely on rack.

Makes 8 to 10 servings

Index